# Key To Deep Change

**Diligently Adding to Your Faith**

**2 Peter 1:3-11**

# Discipling Intensive #2

# Leader's Guide

Dr. Steve Smith

©2025 by Steve Smith

ISBN: 978-1-941000-25-0

All rights reserved. No part of this publication may be reproduced, stored in a retrieval system, or transmitted in any form or by any means, electronic, mechanical, photocopy recording, or any other—except for brief quotations in printed reviews, without prior permission of the authors.

www.ChurchEquippers.com

All Scripture quotations, unless otherwise indicated, are taken from the Holy Bible, New International Version®, NIV®. Copyright ©1973, 1978, 1984, 2011 by Biblica, Inc.™ Used by permission of Zondervan. All rights reserved worldwide. www.zondervan.com The "NIV" and "New International Version" are trademarks registered in the United States Patent and Trademark Office by Biblica, Inc.™

## Contents

Instructions for the Leader ................................. 1
Introduction to Do Disciplines ........................... 7
Session 1: Diligently Adding to Your Faith ........ 11
Session 2: Being Filled with the Spirit ............... 21
Session 3 - Do Discipline 1: Goodness .............. 29
Session 4 - Do Discipline 2: Knowledge ........... 39
Session 5 - Do Discipline 3: Self-control .......... 47
Session 6 - Do Discipline 4: Perseverance ........ 55
Session 7 - Do Discipline 5: Godliness .............. 63
Session 8 - Do Discipline 6: Mutual Affection ... 73
Session 9 - Do Discipline 7: Love ....................... 83
Session 10 – Effective and Productive ............. 91

## Instructions for the Leader

Thank you for being willing to help others on their faith journey by facilitating this intensive of the Do Disciplines. I hope that this experience will also help you on your own journey as you lead people to discover how to actively engage in growing in their faith.

Like the *Key to Deep Change Discipling Intensive*, Do Disciplines is not designed to be a Bible study but a process. Those participating in this experience build on the three essential truths we learned in the previous intensive. The first truth is the intimacy we have been gaining by being with God through the Done Disciplines of Rest, Appropriation, and Meditating on Christ's love. The second is the transformation taking place in their lives due to the empowering presence of the Spirit, who has been given to them by God. The Spirit is the sign of the new covenant that we enter when we put our faith in Jesus. The third is our experience living in a confessing community with other believers.

In these ten sessions, we are discipling believers, showing them how to actively engage with God in the process of being conformed into Jesus' likeness. The key word is 'actively.' God, who freely entered into covenant with us, does not expect us to be passive in our faith journey. He has empowered us by the Spirit within to join Him in our transformational process. What this intensive does is make plain the practices that will strengthen a believer in this pursuit.

These sessions are mainly based on 2 Peter 1:3-11. In this passage, Peter has combined the basic truths of God's transformational work with our active engagement in growing in grace. It is of the utmost importance that those being discipled see the connection between these two truths. It will prevent us from believing that transformation is our job instead of God's. Adding to our faith is an empowered response, allowing disciples to become what we were created to be instead of trying to become a pale imitation of what we are in Christ.

The **bolded sentences** in the sessions are only found in the leader's guide. These notes are here to inform you what you are looking for in the answers the participants give. When their answers do not line up with these truths, you will need to use the notes to help them grasp important truths.

## Basic Guidelines for Leading a Group Study

Do not allow believers who have not already taken the Key to Deep Change discipling intensive to participate in this second intensive. Lacking the understanding of the empowering work of the Spirit and their need to allow God to heal and free their hearts first will most probably send them off in the wrong direction with the Do Disciplines. Encourage them to go through the first intensive instead of trying to attend the second one. Then, the second intensive will make sense and be attainable for them.

While the Key to Deep Change discipling intensive #1 required that the group be men with men or women with women only, it is possible to offer mixed groups in this intensive. If you choose to do this, be aware that some of the homework asks the participants to discuss temptations they struggle against. This may cause some discomfort and limit honest talk.

It is also important that the group size be an interactive size, no more than ten if possible, so that all the participants will be able to speak during the sessions. Larger groups allow people to hide and avoid sharing when faced with tough truths. Be firm in saying 'No' to people who want to join when you reach a workable size group.

Each of the ten sessions contains different foundational truths that are included to lead the participants forward in their faith journey. Each session builds on the truths of the previous one. The participants are offered the opportunity to apply these truths to their relationship with God. Start each session with prayer that points to this reality. Then, lead them interactively through all the questions for the session you are in. It is important to finish if at all possible, so schedule at least one and a half hours for each session.

Unlike Key to Deep Change, Do Disciplines requires more teaching on your part. While there are reflective questions in each session, it is necessary for you to supply scriptural insights that may be hidden from the participants at this moment. All the information you will need to teach these insights is in your Leader's Guide. Feel free to supplement the answers with your own knowledge of God and Scripture.

Each session is designed to take 60-75 minutes. Except for the first and last session, there is homework to be done by the participants that will allow them to practice each discipline they learn. The group will talk about their homework at the beginning of each session. This is an accountability tool to encourage them to immediately practice what they learn. Otherwise, it will be easy for them to never actually engage with the Do Disciplines.

At times, people need to process out loud what they are learning in class. We have found that there are times when the leader will need to allow people to take their time when they begin to process, which may mean that the session will take longer than planned. Because this is a progressive process—teaching people spiritual disciplines, each one built on what was learned in the previous session—do not skip over the material that you might not be able to finish within the proposed time frame. If you have to extend the session to finish, do so. Do not add the unanswered questions to the next study. In other words, let them learn and practice each new truth as completely as they can before they are faced with the next spiritual truth. However, if the need to extend sessions becomes a habit of your group, reevaluate the size of your group for the next class. You may also need to take steps to better guide the interaction to keep people from overtalking.

To lead this study effectively, you will need to embrace four practices that make it work. The first is transparency, which is a result of growing in grace. For you to have credibility in your leadership, you must openly talk about your own journey—how God changed you as you practiced these disciplines. Transparency tells those you will guide in this process that there is zero difference between you and them. It also offers them hope—that if God can change your life, He can set them free also.

The second is to teach without lecturing. There are a lot of questions and reflective work in this study. You need to avoid filling in the blanks for them, answering the questions with which they need to grapple. Be sure to know what the answers are yourself and point them in the right direction if they get stuck. But if you find you are focused only on what *you* want to say for each question instead of listening to the participants, in time you will kill the group or at least lessen the learning that could have taken place.

The third is to allow them time to self-discover. Not all will move forward at the same pace or even understand at the same level what is being learned. Be okay with that instead of trying to play the role of the Holy Spirit in leading them to truth.

The fourth and final practice is to always be guiding the participants towards God. You cannot make anyone grow up in their faith, so guard your expectations. It is God's Spirit who leads believers to the truth and empowers their practice of the disciplines.

What follows is the *Participant's Guide* interspersed with background information and directions for you in bold print that will help you prepare to lead this study week by week. Every session is built around an expected outcome, stated at the beginning of the session. As you lead each session, seek to keep the participants on track so that this outcome can be achieved. Use humor and kindness to assert their need to stay on course, assuring them that the cumulative effect of the sessions will deepen their spiritual life with God.

One final piece of advice: If you have someone in the group who wants to dominate the conversation, overtalks in sessions, and always draws the group into his or her personal ideas about the disciplines, take the time to talk with this person apart from the group. Ask the person to practice self-control. If that person continues to seek to control the group's focus, this is an indication of a pride issue in his or her life. It may be necessary to ask that person to step out of the group and seek private counseling with a spiritual counselor. Do not hesitate to choose the group's needs over this person.

**Explanation of the Text of 2 Peter 1:3-11**

I have slightly edited by the text of 2 Peter 1:3-11 for this study. It cannot be found in any Bible translation as it is worded in this discipling intensive, although the words I chose are used in different versions. The two words I chose to use are 'goodness' and 'diligent'.

Goodness is used in verses 3 and 5. It refers to God's divine nature. He is good in Himself. Because this is true, we are enjoined by Peter to add goodness to our faith. I chose to use the word 'goodness' over two other ways the Greek word is translated in other versions—'virtue' and 'moral excellence'. While all these words refer to the same thing, I felt goodness was a warmer word and more relatable to those who will take this intensive than the other two. But to be clear, goodness is not something God gained, but what God *is*. Therefore, He cannot act otherwise. For a believer to add goodness is to continually be being restored in the image of God.

The choice to use the word 'diligent' in verses 5 and 10 was to capture Peter's sense of urgency. He is not merely *reminding* us we need to be actively engaged in this task. He is *pressing* us to do so.

It is my desire to highlight these two aspects of the passage. You will see them in the first session. Therefore, as the believers you are discipling read from their varying Bible translations, be sure to point out the use of these words in the sessions so they will not be confused when their version says it differently.

## Introduction to Do Disciplines

This is the follow-up discipling intensive for you who are already learning to pursue intimacy with God, learning to surrender your unfinished business to Him so you can be healed and delivered. In the Key to Deep Change Discipling Intensive #1, you were trained in spiritual warfare and how to keep in step with the Spirit.

It is a critical issue for disciples to *continue*. Continue to abide in Christ. Continue to grow in grace and the knowledge of Jesus. Continue on your journey of being transformed so you will be productive and effective in your faith. You do not want to stay where you were when God saved you. You need to go on.

One way you can get stuck and stop moving forward is when you make your unfinished business the narrative of your life instead of making God the story. You continue to worry about it, concerned that you might be someone who does not get well. You can mistakenly order your life around your hurts and your need to stop sinning. You find yourself doubting you are spiritually ready to be used by God. This is a faith issue that the enemy exploits. You want to make your relationship with God the growing narrative of your life. Focus on Him. Then He will take care of your unfinished business as you trust Him more, finding yourself surrendering to Him more because you are living securely in His love.

This discipling intensive will guide you further in your spiritual growth by introducing you to the Do Disciplines. Practicing them will allow you to actively pursue growing in grace. The power for this has already been given to you in the person of the Spirit. These Do Disciplines are contained in Peter's challenge for his readers in his second letter to 'add to their faith' a list of seven characteristics:

goodness, knowledge, self-control, perseverance, godliness, mutual affection, and love.

What does 'Do Disciplines' mean? A discipline is a necessary spiritual exercise that God uses to change you deeply as you practice it. Eventually, they will become natural spiritual actions on your part.

These seven are called 'Do' in contrast to 'Done.' When you practice Done Disciplines, you are gaining greater understanding of what God has done for you already in Christ. You learn to rest from your own works and be with God to know Him better. You appropriate what He has already given you. You meditate on Christ's agape love so you can grasp how wide, high, long, and deep it is. These practices deepen your trust and intimacy with God.

Do Disciplines are those you practice in cooperation with God's work in you. Peter instructs us to diligently practice these. But it is not merely about *what* you do. It is about *who you are being revealed to be* as you practice these disciplines. Many Christians attempt to 'do' their faith as if it is a task to be accomplished. The Do Disciplines will challenge you to embrace the godly character that is Christ's.

These disciplines are drawn from Peter's words in 2 Peter 1:5-8. Briefly, they are:

**Goodness:** The practice of forming your character based on God's character as revealed in Jesus' life, putting to death sin in your flesh by the Spirit.

**Knowledge:** The practice of studying God's Word in order to know God's character better.

**Self-Control:** The practice of saying 'No' to ungodliness and worldly passions.

**Perseverance:** The practice of steadfastness in the face of temptation and discouragement.

**Godliness:** The practice of focusing your heart on what God wants you to do.

**Mutual Affection:** The practice of meeting the physical, emotional, and spiritual needs of those who belong to Jesus' family.

**Love:** The practice of choosing to actively love those outside the faith, even those who hate and persecute you.

This is the 'putting on Christ' aspect of faith living. It means you will find yourself changed from the inside out to be the person God predestined you to be, according to Romans 8:29. What Peter's 'adding to your faith' challenge does *not* mean is that you are now going to reform yourself to be like Jesus by your own effort. He means you are active participants with God in the process of restoration. You should not be passive about who you are in Christ, but eager to become right now what you will be revealed to be when you stand before Him.

This discipling intensive is not a Bible study, informing you about what each of the characteristics means. From the start you will be taught to depend on the Spirit's power and continually be being filled by him so that these seven practices are realized in your life. Every session prepares you for the next, as Peter intended for each of these practices to strengthen the one before it.

It will probe you to help uncover where you may not now be conformed in these areas, show you what to examine personally, and guide you in what to choose to practice by the Spirit's power.

You will be prepared to keep walking forward with God and not stay at the starting gate of faith. It will help you become effective and productive as His children in proclaiming the truth of the gospel through your life.

The central goal of this discipling intensive is to help you deepen your intimacy with God so you will live out His will with your life. This is what being His child means. You were created to be in relationship with Him. That relationship cannot help but change you deeply and make you a more devoted worshipper of your Father and Creator.

Here is your challenge: to complete this intensive. To neither become distracted with other interests nor be discouraged from your need for more growth so that you quit. These outcomes are the work of the enemy. God has purposed for you to take this time so you can grow in His grace. Be steadfast! Encourage others with you to be steadfast. Confess when you feel weak. Pray for each other. And see what God will do because you followed through to the end.

One final note. You will gain much more out of this discipling intensive by investing time to do the weekly homework. As well as the assignments at the end of each session, this homework includes prepping yourself by looking up the Scripture used in the upcoming session and thinking through the next questions. This allows you to better participate and ask questions that might have come to you as you prepared.

# Session 1: Diligently Adding to Your Faith

> *Goal of this Session: I choose to be diligent in adding to my faith because I have already been given everything I need to live this righteous life through my experiential knowledge of God.*

**2 Peter 1:5 "For this very reason, be diligent to add to your faith."**

1. What are some benefits you personally have already gained in pursuing intimacy with God through the Done Disciplines?

   **Those taking this course should have already completed the *Key to Deep Change Discipling Intensive #1* as a prerequisite. This question is to connect the two intensives. Use it to discover how well they are doing in pursuing intimacy with God.**

2. What do you expect you will gain through this training in the Do Disciplines?

   **Expect every participant to answer. If no one mentions this, explain to them that a relationship with God is a mutual one—God is transforming them, but they also get to participate with God in the process empowered by the Spirit. This is the basis of sanctification by faith—being saved from the power of sin.**

3. We are going to take an in-depth look at 2 Peter 1:3-11. Note how many places in this passage Peter speaks about our part in our spiritual journey.

**Read this passage for the group. Have them identify every place (underlined and bolded) that Peter speaks about the believer's part in growing in their faith.**

*His divine power has given us everything we need for a godly life through our knowledge of him who called us by his own glory and goodness. Through these he has given us his very great and precious promises,* **<u>so that through them you may participate in the divine nature,</u>** *having escaped the corruption in the world caused by evil desires. For this very reason,* **<u>be diligent to add to your faith</u>** *goodness; and to goodness, knowledge; and to knowledge, self-control; and to self-control, perseverance; and to perseverance, godliness; and to godliness, mutual affection; and to mutual affection, love.* **<u>For if you possess these qualities in increasing measure, they will keep you from being ineffective and unproductive in your knowledge of our Lord Jesus Christ</u>**. *But whoever does not have them is nearsighted and blind, forgetting that they have been cleansed from their past sins.* **<u>Therefore, my brothers and sisters, be diligent to confirm your calling and election</u>**. *For* **<u>if you do these things</u>**, *you will never stumble, and you will receive a rich welcome into the eternal kingdom of our Lord and Savior Jesus Christ.*

- Examine some of the very great and precious promises that Peter is speaking about that make our faith journey possible.

    **Have the participants read these passages out loud in the group. Quiz them on how much these promises mean to them.**

    o  Everlasting life (John 3:16)

- - No one can take you out of his hands (John 10:28)
  - Abide in me and you will bear much fruit. (John 15:5-8)
  - Unity, love and presence (John 17:20-23)
  - Spirit in you – another comforter (John 14:16-17)
  - In this world you will have tribulation. But take heart because I've overcome the world. (John 16:33)
  - I will be with you to the end of the age. (Matthew 28:20)
- Who is teaching us these promises?

  **Jesus. This is a reminder of who is our main teacher of the faith.**

- How do these promises make it possible to participate in the divine nature and escape the corruption of this world caused by evil desires? Do you sense you have grasped this for yourself?

  **'Evil desires' is the biblical term for the deadly or motivational sins. Escaping the corruption of this world is not a passive act on the part of believers but requires us to actively resist because we have been given the power to do so by God. Share 1 Peter 5:8-9 with them for added confirmation of this.**

- What do you do about evil desires?

  **Evil desires are inherently part of being affected by the Fall. The sanctification process is saving you from their power as you surrender them to God, who will replace them with a righteous character formed by the Spirit.**

4. The practical nature of the gospel is summed up in Romans 8:29.

   - What do you understand is your proper response to this process of being conformed to the likeness of Jesus?

   **To actively add to your faith. This is where this discipling intensive will help them.**

   - Connect your answer to the following statement: *Now with God's help, I will become myself.* -Soren Kierkegaard. Do you think this statement is compatible or contradictory to Romans 8:29? Why or why not?

   **There is real confusion in the minds of believers about obedience. Obedience does not lead to a believer's transformation. Instead, transformation leads to the believer's increasing obedience to the will of the Father. But as a believer becomes more like Jesus, he or she is becoming what they were created to be from the beginning. This is what Kierkegaard means about becoming oneself, living out empowered freedom unencumbered with the baggage of unfinished business caused by unhealed hurt and the weight of sin.**

5. Becoming yourself involves living as a kingdom servant. What does that involve according to the following verses: John 14:15; Ephesians 4:20-24; Romans 8:12; Romans 13:14; 1 Timothy 4:7-8.

   **Deliberately seeking to put on Christ—a phrase that means to imitate his character—because you no longer desire to live your life in damaging ways.**

"If you love me, keep my commands." This statement is followed directly by Jesus promising to send the Spirit to his disciples. In other words, obedience here is not uncoupled with the Spirit's power.

"Therefore, brothers and sisters, we have an obligation—but it is not to the flesh, to live according to it." This verse points to the New Covenant. All covenants make obligations of the parties involved. God obligated Himself to write His law on our hearts and minds and to remember our sins no more. Our obligation is simple, by the power of the Spirit, we are not to live according to the flesh, i.e. continue to sin.

1 Timothy 4:7-8 will come up again in this session and in Session 7.

- What challenge do they reveal about growing as a believer?

    These verses are a challenge to the will of the believer—will I do this or not? This is exactly why continually dealing with unfinished business is a necessary part of the sanctification process. If a believer allows his or her damaged emotions to determine how to live out the faith, they will continually be compromised and confused by their lack of godliness. Instead, by choosing to be whole, they get life, and life abundantly, as Jesus promised.

- How do you reconcile these challenges to the truth that God is the one who transforms you?

    We are always in danger of believing that, because God is the one who changes us from the inside out, the person on a faith journey is just to surrender passively to God's powerful work—God does it all and we just watch. But

**God continually reminds us in Scripture to actively pursue the holy life that faith in Jesus has delivered to us.**

- Do you ever feel concerned or maybe disappointed about what kind of person you are as a believer? Why? Where does your disappointment come from?

**This leads to the danger of trying harder to please God instead of drawing closer to God. To focus on the task instead of the relationship. If we become successful in the flesh by working hard at it, pride robs us. Satan is the accuser and much of our disappointment comes from his lies. On the other hand, we might be being slack in our pursuit of God, feeling adrift from His empowering presence.**

- How do the truths found in Romans 8:1-4, 31-39 counter any thoughts you may have that God is disappointed with you?

**There is no condemnation because God knows we could never become ourselves and live obediently apart from His grace. Yet, all the time we are on this journey, stumbling along, having to repent and confess and get back on track, He never changes His stance towards us, never accepts Satan's accusations against us, withholds nothing we need, or stops loving us according to His covenant.**

6. What does Peter mean when he speaks about faith?

**Faith can be about a set of beliefs, but Peter means more than affirming the right things about God. He means trusting God and walking in intimacy with Him.**

- How does this connect with Romans 1:17?

   **Faith is never the focus by itself, as in "have faith in faith." Faith always must be directed at an object. Paul is not saying, "The just will live by having faith." but "by faith." Meaning they are to have faith in the one who is able to make them righteous, that is, God or the Faithful One.**

- Read Hebrews 11:1, 6 to expand your understanding about faith.

   **This is what faith is all about. We have chosen to come to God, believing that he is and that he is a rewarder of those who diligently seek him. Faith is a way of knowing. It requires that we act on something because we know what is true → that God is and He is a rewarder of those who diligently seek Him.**

- Why are you challenged to add to your faith?

   **If you believe God is really who He says He is, then you want your life to realign with His in every way. This is the basic definition of righteousness.**

7. Examine these seven practices that you are to add to your faith. In which ones do you feel you are currently doing well? In which ones do you know you need to be more diligent?

   **Give them time to reflect before answering.**

   - Goodness: Actively seek to put on the character of Jesus, empowered by the Spirit to put to death sin in you.

   - Knowledge: Discover through the revealed word and intimacy with Him, who God is.

- Self-control: Say 'No' to the pull of addictive behaviors.

- Perseverance: Continue to live out goodness even when it is hard and people oppose you.

- Godliness: Live life with a heart focused on what God wants for you and through you.

- Mutual affection: Care for the needs of others in your family of faith.

- Love: Actively love those outside the faith, even those who hate and persecute you.

**This last can be trying, which is why it is a discipline.**

8. Consider the following statement by Watchman Nee: *The all-important rule is not to 'try' but to 'trust', not to depend on our own strength but upon his. Too many of us are caught acting as Christians.*

- Have you ever been told "Fake it until you make it." by someone teaching you about following Jesus? Why is this not a good model for growing in grace?

**'Faking it' means you are trying in your own strength to be a Christian. You are doomed to fail at this effort and it will frustrate you even to the point of feeling like abandoning the faith.**

- What is the difference between trying and trusting?

**God has already given us everything we need for life and godliness. Trying can lead to frustration and failure because we lack personal strength to be good for God. We quit things because we don't see the value of it.**

- Read 1 Timothy 4:7-8 and 2 Timothy 1:6-9. How does trusting challenge you to enter into training?

    **If you knew without a doubt you were going to succeed, then as tough as the preparation is, you would want to do it. This is true for the *zoe* life God has given you. You will win without a doubt, so being diligent to train is worth it.**

9. The biblical word 'training' means 'going to the gym.'

    - What might this tell you about why Peter chose the word diligent to challenge his disciples?

        **Spiritual strength, like physical strength, is built up over time as you exercise it. You have to be diligent, regularly practicing these disciplines, or you will get indifferent results.**

    - What does diligence look like in connection to adding to your faith?

        **Regular and consistent practice so that they become a natural and habitual part of your person.**

    - In verses 8-9, Peter mentions some serious consequences for not being diligent. Why do you think people fail to be diligent?

        **Therefore, my brothers and sisters, make every effort to confirm your calling and election. This is not a sprint, but a marathon. Lifelong pursuit. Practicing these disciplines is a confirmation that you are truly in covenant with God (v10). You are not merely 'playing the game' of being a 'Christian' but have real faith.**

**10.** End this session with encouragement for the participants to choose to be diligent. Choosing is the only 'power' you have, but by choosing, the person becomes an active partner with God in the transformational process. If you choose to diligently add to your faith, God will empower you to do what He made you to do. It doesn't mean it will be easy – it will sometimes challenge you at tough moments.

**Homework:** Read through the next session, looking up all the verses mentioned and thinking through the questions. This is a repeated assignment for all future sessions.

# Session 2: Being Filled with the Spirit

> *Goal of this Session: I will pursue being continually filled with the Spirit to be able to pursue gaining the characteristics of a mature follower (putting on Christ).*

**Ephesians 5:18 "Instead, be filled with the Spirit."**

1. What did Jesus teach his disciples about this issue: John 1:14; John 3:34; Luke 11:13.

   **Jesus was full of grace and truth. Grace is the empowering presence of God's Spirit, which was also given to all who believe.**

   - Why should it matter to you what Jesus is and teaches?

   **We do as our Rabbi does—not just say or act like him, but live his life by the Spirit's power.**

2. Review this illustration from the Key to Deep Change Discipling Intensive.

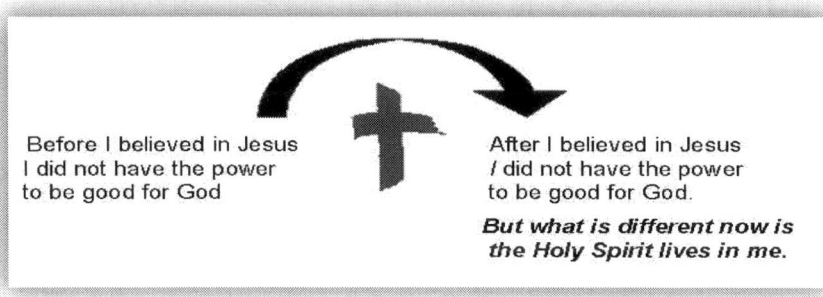

- What does this illustration show you about living out your faith?

  **It reminds us that, just as before we believed we had no power in ourselves to be good, neither do we have it in ourselves now to be good. But now we have the Spirit, who has been given us by God so we can live righteously. This will also help bridge the participants' connection between the two discipling intensives.**

3. Read Acts 2:37-39.

   - How do you know that you have the promised Holy Spirit?

     **This is a prophetic promise of God from Joel 2:28, initiated on the Day of Pentecost for all who believe.** *"And afterward, I will pour out my Spirit on all people. Your sons and daughters will prophesy, your old men will dream dreams, your young men will see visions."*

   - Here are the reasons why God gave us the Spirit:

     **Make sure to read each verse out loud in the session**

     o Covenantal reason: Romans 8:15-16

        **Covenant is about deep unbreakable relationship. All covenants include a sign signifying the completion of the covenant. The Spirit is the sign of the New Covenant. See Ephesians 1:13.**

     o Revelational reason: Ephesians 6:18; John 14:26; John 16:13-16

        **The purpose of revelation is to understand what God is saying to us.**

     o Church body reason: 1 Corinthians 12:7

- **Equipping people for ministry for the good of the church family.**

  o Missional reason: Acts 1:8; 1 Thessalonians 1:5

  **Empowering believers to be witnesses to everyone who needs to the gospel.**

  o Transformational reason; Romans 5:5, Galatians 5:22-23

  **God's purpose is to transform us into the character of Jesus.**

  o Summarize what these reasons tell you into a single sentence.

  **God has given us His Spirit so we can live the life God has given us in Christ in all its aspects, because God knew we could not do this in our own power.**

  o How have you already experienced the power of the Spirit in your relationship with God?

  **Encourage all to respond to this. If there is confusion or some frustration expressed, explore what they have been taught about the Spirit since becoming a follower of Jesus. Many believers do not have a deep understanding of the Spirit in spite of him being the sign of the new covenant.**

4. Read the following statement.

   *Watchman Nee taught that Ephesians could be divided into three sections—sit, walk, stand. 'Sit' refers to the teachings of chapters 1-3, where we are reminded that God raised us up with Christ by grace and seated us at His right hand in Christ in the heavenly places. All three chapters point to what God has done for us in Christ. In chapter 4:1-6:9, Paul teaches us about how we are to live out our faith, using the term 'walk' over and over again—walk worthy, differently than we did before, in love, light and wisdom. In the third section, 6:10-18, Paul uses the word 'stand' to teach about spiritual warfare. What is important to know is that both the 'walk' and 'stand' sections are dependent on the reality of us 'sitting.' We do not 'move on' to the other things when we finish chapters 1-3, we find we are able to walk and stand because we are seated at God's right hand in Christ."*

*Most Christians make the mistake of trying to walk in order to sit, but that is the reversal of the true order. Our natural reason says, If we do not walk, how will we ever reach the goal? What can we attain without effort? How can we ever get anywhere if we do not move? But Christianity is a strange business! If at the outset we try to do anything, we get nothing; if we seek to attain something, we miss everything. For Christianity begins not with a big DO, but with a big DONE."* -Watchman Nee

- What is the connection between the gift of the Spirit and adding to your faith?

  **All that you will add to your faith is only possible by the empowering work of the Spirit. The goal of this intensive is not that you will work at being good, knowledgeable, self-controlled, etc., but that you will naturally be that kind of person as you actively embrace who you are in Christ.**

- How can you tell the difference between flesh driven obedience and Spirit led obedience in this area?

  **Flesh driven efforts are the product of one of three motivations: fear, duty or pride. Some try to be good for God so He will not punish them. Others try to be good for God because they are supposed to as a Christian. Still others find it's 'easy' to be good for God and just**

**do it. Discuss these three with the group. Guide them in recognizing which one is most likely to trip each person up.**

- All of the Do Disciplines are rooted in the reality of being filled with the Spirit. If your growth in faith is dependent on the power of the Spirit, how can you be sure you are actually operating in his power?

  **All the other approaches lack a true sense of dependency, humility, and gratitude to God, which is the characteristic of Spirit-led obedience. Look to see what God is producing in these areas as each moves forward with the Do Disciplines. Stress that this is why we learn the Done Disciplines first, so we will comprehend the realness of God and His Spirit. Otherwise, what you are learning here would be only informative instead of transformative.**

5. Read Ephesians 5:18-20. What is Paul's point in contrasting getting drunk and being filled with the Spirit?

   **Compare this to Acts 2:1-13 (disciples accused of being drunk on the day of Pentecost). There is a healthy emotional component to being filled that people notice, emotions that even can be to the point of levity /hilarity due to the great joy it produces in God. Levity is not the everyday norm—think of Jesus. But being filled by the Spirit does mean he controls you in the same way that alcohol can control a person, guiding and enabling you to do what would not be normal, albeit in the way of righteousness and wholeness instead of damage and shame.**

   - What are the outcomes that Paul says indicate filling?

     **Worship of and gratitude to God.**

- Why are these the outcomes to look for?

    **If these are showing up in your life, this indicates the Spirit's filling.**

- What does continually being filled mean for you?

    **Continually being is not a one-time event. There is a consciousness necessary for this journey, an investment and awareness of the Spirit. It is important to point out that this filling is an imperative verb—a command to carry out made possible by the very Spirit we are commanded to be filled by!**

- What might hinder being filled by the Spirit, according to Ephesians 4:29-31?

    **We can grieve the Spirit by continuing in anger and division in the body of Christ. We should desire to get rid of this out of our life—again by the power of the Spirit himself!**

6. Here is how do you consciously embrace being filled.

    **Guide them through this section.**

    - Ask God daily. Luke 11:9-13 "How much more will your Father in heaven give the Holy Spirit to those who ask him!"

        **Don't put God in a box! Often, we can only imagine him doing "this" much (the amount that fits in that box). Ask, "Am I missing out on something, God?" Ask to experience everything God has for us as believers. Acts 4:23-3. What will hold you back in asking is sin.**

    - Believe.

He is not tricking us with snakes and scorpions! Believe that He is a good Father who truly wants the best for you, including filling you with His empowering presence. Warn the participants to beware of emotionalism, meaning that the trust their good feelings to tell them the Spirit is present in their lives. Instead, the Spirit's presence is real even when they feel bad about themselves. Remind them that the enemy can lie to them through their emotions. Encourage them that them can trust God's truth no matter what they feel.

- Obey.

    Go forward trusting that God is empowering you as He promised.

- Notice.

    This filling is about deepening your relationship with God. Is that the outcome you are seeing?

- Repeat.

    Remember that God is the one who fills you—this is being done <u>to</u> you.

**Homework:** Spend time each morning before your day gets busy and ask God to fill you afresh with His Holy Spirit. **Suggest a prayer you use. Or share this one: Father, thank you for including me in your kingdom and giving me the Spirit. Today I ask that you fill me again with his power. Open my mind to hear the truths he will show me. Amen.**

# Session 3: Do Discipline 1: Goodness

> *Goal of this Session: I will look to God's character as what I should be, willingly putting off my old self, and instead be empowered to put on the goodness of God.*

**2 Peter 1:5 "add to your faith goodness."**

1. Review Homework: What have you learned about being continually filled with the Spirit so far?

   **Encourage each participant to answer. Being filled by the Spirit is not a Do Discipline but it is the foundation of their ability to do any of the disciplines.**

2. Why do you believe that Peter urges his readers to add to their faith the discipline of goodness?

   **Young believers can be content in just having faith and belonging to the church. But true faith is active and pushes us to intentionally pursue a godly character.**

3. To understand goodness, we must start with understanding what the Fall has done to us. Read Romans 1:13-32 and Galatians 5:19-21.

   - Why did Paul make these observations?

   **The original people reading the letter practiced such things before they placed their faith in Jesus and were justified. These sins continue to plague humanity, including us.**

- What are the human results of the Fall, according to Paul?

  **These results are in the verses, which are the hard outcome of the work of the flesh.**

- In what ways do you see yourself in this list?

  **Remind the participants that this is not an exercise in shame and guilt, but an opportunity to recognize what God has saved them from, similar to 1 Corinthians 6:11.** *And that is what some of you were. But you were washed, you were sanctified, you were justified in the name of the Lord Jesus Christ and by the Spirit of our God.*

- What have these sins done to family relationships, including yours?

  **Encourage the participants to explore this in depth.**

- What have these sins done to the relationships between cultures?

  **Make sure they include the loss of mercy and justice in the world. All cultures have been built by people affected by the Fall, so there are no God-honoring cultures, although godly people live throughout the world.**

4. All who have put their faith in Jesus know that God's character is different from the fallen world's ideas about Him. But what is meant by the biblical idea that "God is good." (Psalm 136:1)?

   **It is not just that God is good in some supportive, loving way. It means the very definition of righteousness is God—nothing He does or will do is out of character with good. He acts in a consistent manner that is praiseworthy as a way of**

existence instead of choosing to be virtuous in the moment. And He does not desire to act any other way. This is true even when we wonder how what we are experiencing under His rule could be called good. This word is also translated from the Greek into English as virtue or moral excellence.

- How does this truth, "God is good." challenge us in regard to our personal knowledge of good and evil?

    **God is good, so anything in us that is not like God is evil.**

- How does the world get goodness wrong?

    **All cultures built by people are affected by the Fall.**

- How does religion get goodness wrong?

    **Religion sees goodness as morality, as something we do to please God instead of goodness as our character formed by the Spirit as we spend time in intimacy with God.**

5. What did Jesus teach his disciples about this issue: Parable from Matthew 20:1-16.

    **The Bible uses two parallel words to speak of goodness: 1) *agathos* - goodness of character; 2) *arete* - the outward display of goodness, that is, doing life with excellence and honor. 2 Peter uses the latter term. Here Jesus uses the first.**

    - This is a parable about the kingdom, which is Jesus' way of speaking about God's reign over His creation. What is Jesus revealing about the Kingdom?

        **All who acknowledge God's reign will be treated with the same compassion, whether they came in at the last**

minute of their lives or spent their entire existence in His service.

- How was this man good?

    **He was impartial in his response to the needs of the workers. All were treated equally in their needs, including those who were the first to be hired.**

- Why didn't everyone in the parable think he was good?

    **This is one attribute of God many people do not understand, His impartiality. Because of the Fall, believers find themselves thinking they are competing for love, seeing it as a transaction instead of transformation. "I worked harder for you, God, so I deserve more!" Impartiality means He loves us all well. Unfortunately, not all believers are grateful as a result.**

- How is this man's goodness meant to reveal God's goodness?

    **God's goodness is consistent with his own definition of good rather than what someone He created might define as good.**

6. Notice the use of goodness in 2 Peter 1:3 and 5. How is God's goodness the model of the goodness that we are to add to our faith?

    **Because of the close connection of thought between verse 3 and 5, it is clear that Peter is linking God's goodness to our goodness, as an aspect of our being in His image. Because we were created in the image of God, it is His purpose to**

restore us in our own goodness by conforming us to the likeness of Jesus as stated in Romans 8:29.

- The word used to describe God's character is 'attributes.' This word is used to signify that God, unlike humans, did not develop His character, but that He always was, is and will be these attributes. What do the following attributes contribute to our understanding of God's goodness?

    **God has many attributes, attributes of both His infinite powers, like omnipotence, omnipresence, and omniscience, and His personhood. These are not something He acquired. These are who He is. His personhood attributes are what He put into us when He created us in His image and are seen in us through the restorative work of Jesus' death and the active presence of the Spirit in us. When we speak the word 'good,' we are speaking of God being Himself. This is because He defines good in Himself, and so His actions are always good, even when we struggle to understand Him. If we are becoming like God, we are becoming good.**

    o Kind.

    **How He acts towards His people, even when they do not deserve it.**

    o Merciful.

    **His willingness to forgive instead of giving us the judgment we so richly deserve when we disobey Him.**

    o Love.

The love that is produced by His desire and will for us and for the whole world, leading Him to send Jesus into the world to pay the death penalty of all who have been affected by the Fall if they put their faith in Jesus.

- Patient.

    His ability to wait to act until it is the right time and the person or group who is the object of His patience is ready to complete His will.

- Joyful.

    His unbounded gladness of heart about Himself and his people and all that He does.

- Compassionate.

    His ability to act on behalf of the broken, oppressed and hurting, to bring them to wholeness.

- Righteous.

    He always does what is right because He is. The definition of righteous is God—He cannot act otherwise.

- Impartial.

    God prefers His own plans, so He treats all His creation the same. This does not mean He therefore cannot choose or must save all. It means He will do His will without advice from those he created.

- Faithful.

> **God cannot lie. He will do what He has sworn, based on two unchangeable things—His character and His word.**

- Do you see yourself possessing these attributes? Why or why not?

  **Give them time to process. Remind them that this is why God set his will ahead of time (predestined) to conform us to Jesus' likeness. This is our restoration back to being in the image of God.**

7. Read Galatians 5:16-18 and Ephesians 4:20-22.

   - What are we to do as believers to discipline ourselves in goodness?

     **We are to keep in step with—pay attention to—the Spirit. This also means we are to allow the Spirit to address our inner attitude so that it will be aligned with God's righteousness and holiness.**

8. How do you practice the discipline of goodness?

   - In keeping with Paul's teaching in Romans 8:13, determine to put sin in your flesh to death by the Spirit. This is a trust step—believing that he is truly within you and is powerfully able to kill sin in your flesh in a way that you are powerless to do. This involves several actions on your part:
     - Intentionally listen to the Spirit about what you do, think, or believe that is not in keeping with the character of Jesus. This should be a regular part of your

conversation with God. Pay attention also to what the Spirit reveals as you read Scripture.

**Being transformed into the likeness of Jesus is a lifelong journey that challenges us to examine ourselves in light of the Spirit's work to lead us to all truth.**

- Explore your heart to discover where these symptoms are coming from.

  **Review the Heart Chart in class. Remind them that all that is not in keeping with Jesus' character is coming from our heart. Share with them symptoms you have discovered on your own journey that you took to God in order to discover where they were coming from. This part needs to be more personal, not just informational.**

- Humbly surrender to Jesus the hurts and *sin in me* choices you discover in your heart for healing and deliverance.

  **We need to know the root of our unfinished business in order to surrender what does not belong in our hearts to Jesus. This is an intentional act. Share with them how you talk with God about surrendering your hurt and sin. Tell them what you have experienced.**

- Appropriate the Spirit's power to no longer live that way, but instead live in obedience to Jesus because of your love for him. This should be done with confident faith that God, not you, has actually set you free.

**Appropriating the Spirit's power is a Done Discipline and is also a necessary part of practicing goodness.**

- Repeat.

**Again, remind them that this is a life-long process.**

**Homework:** Review your Heart Chart to see what God wants to deal with in your life right now. Put sin to death by the Spirit, allow God to heal the hurt you discover you have been comforting with sin and walk afresh in freedom and wholeness.

**If you feel the need, revisit the Heart Chart in class to refresh the participants' memory on what it is telling them about what is in their heart and about pursuing intimacy with God to trust Jesus so they will surrender those things to him.**

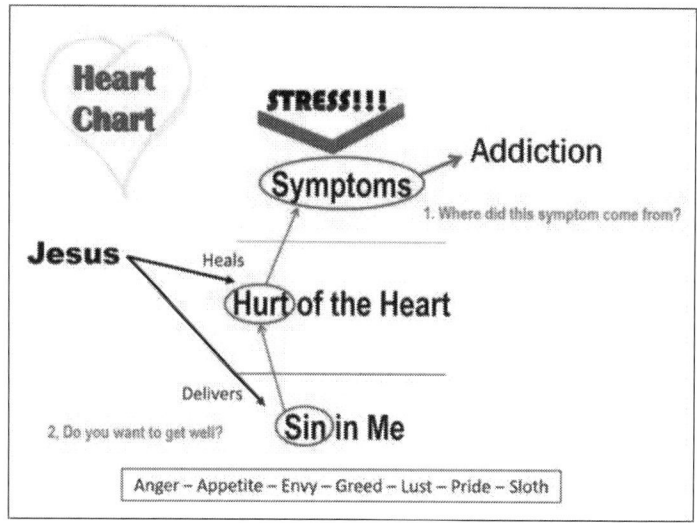

# Session 4: Do Discipline 2: Knowledge

> *Goal of this Session: I will engage in a Spirit-enlightened study process through which I will seek to gain more understanding of God as He has revealed Himself, who Jesus is, His will and purposes in the Bible.*

**2 Peter 1:5 "and to goodness, knowledge."**

1. Review Homework: What have you discovered about adding goodness to your faith so far?

   **Encourage each participant to answer. These sessions are to encourage them to <u>practice</u> the Do Disciplines so they will grow up further in their faith.**

2. The focus of this session is adding the discipline of knowledge to goodness. Note that Peter has already introduced the knowledge of God twice in 1:2-3. What does Ephesians 1:17 reveal about what Peter means by the word 'knowledge' when referring to God?

   **The word means both knowledge gained through insight and through experience so that your relationship with Him grows stronger and deepens. This is different from the idea of knowledge *about* God, as if the goal is to give answers on a test.**

   - In verses 2 & 3 Peter uses the Greek word *epiginosko* to describe how we came to receive all we need for life and godliness from God. In verse 5, Peter uses the related Greek word *ginosko* to show what we need to add to our goodness.

That second word means *to learn to know, come to know, get a knowledge of, to perceive, to feel.*

- How is knowledge here in verse 5 different from knowledge in verse 3?

**Peter uses this word to describe the discipline of knowing God through His revelation of Himself in Scripture. The Bible contains special revelation that God wants us to know about Him by recording how people through the ages experienced Him in relationship.**

- How is the same? How are both references to knowledge the same?

**All knowing comes back to God's desire for us to know Him personally and intimately.**

- If goodness is the character of God, what is the relationship between goodness and this kind of knowledge?

**Gaining insight about God's character and actions (as revealed by God and written down in Scripture) teaches us what we are created to be—and cooperate with the Spirit to become—by setting our hearts on doing so. Furthermore, it increases our knowledge of God will—what He wants us to do as kingdom servants.**

3. Why do we need to be challenged to add this knowledge? Read Romans 1:18-22.

- What has the Fall done to humanity's understanding of God?

**Our ability to know God was totally skewed by the Fall. Human hearts were darkened, meaning we as humans allowed our evil desires to define God from then on.**

- Why do humans replace God with idols?

  **It gives them the false belief that they really know God, manipulating His being into whatever they want Him to be to justify their life choices. This directly runs against the revelation of His divine power and majesty (that is, His right to reign over their lives) and to define what is good and evil.**

- What is the effect of the Fall on people in general in relationship to their knowledge of God?

  **In ignorance, humans have willfully built all of the varying cultures in the world in a way that is completely out of alignment with God's eternal power and divine nature. There is no culture in the world that aligns with the knowledge of God.**

4. Jesus taught about knowledge during his time on earth. Read Matthew 19:3-9; Matthew 22:23-32; John 5:39.

    - What did Jesus teach those who were not disciples about their knowledge of God?

      **Those who do not know God cannot understand God or His revelation of Himself in Scripture. Help them to apply this to popular books written by educated people who claim to debunk the truth of Scripture.**

    - What did Jesus want you as his disciples to understand from these confrontations?

The study of Scripture, even by people who are educated and spend a lot of time at their studies, does not necessarily lead to true understanding of the knowledge of God. Warn the participants that some teachers can lead them astray by misrepresenting God.

- What does it take to really gain insight from Scripture about the knowledge of God according to John 14:26?

**Insight, sometimes called 'illumination,' comes from the Spirit, who has been given to us so we will understand biblical truth and be able to recall Jesus' teaching as it applies to our life situation.**

5. Read also Luke 24:27.

    - What did Jesus teach his disciples about the knowledge of God?

    **Jesus is teaching his disciples that he is the focus of all of Scripture. The purpose of special revelation is God showing us His plan to redeem humans who become reconciled to Him through putting their faith in His Son.**

    **Note: Special revelation is different from general revelation. General revelation is what we can observe about God through His creation. Special revelation is specific truths God showed the writers of the various books included in Scripture that would not have been discernable merely through observation of creation. It includes stories of God's interactions with humans, prophecies He made to and through humans, instructions on how to live out one's faith drawn from the disciples' knowledge of God's character, as well as**

**reflections about God and His righteousness in the Wisdom books of the Old Testament.**

6. Considering what Jesus taught in John 14:8-10 along with Matthew 11:25-27, why then has Scripture been given to us?

   **God is revealing His character (glory) to us through Jesus. Scripture is a revelation of Jesus, who showed us the Father and fulfilled all the prophecies, types, and promises of God. In Him is the fulfillment of the Law, our reconciliation to God's kingdom and the establishment of the Church, of which we are part.**

7. Think about what Paul said in Romans 8:29. Since God has already set His will to conform you to the likeness of Jesus, how does increasing your knowledge of God through Scripture guide you in this process?

   **Guide the participants to grasp what God is specifically doing in them already by the Spirit and how they can cooperate in this transformational process.**

8. How do you do the discipline of knowledge?

   **Tell the participants that this is the introductory level of this discipline. As they grow in maturity, they will want to increase their skills in the study of Scripture.**

   - Study Scripture for yourself: 2 Timothy 3:14-17
     - In what ways will studying Scripture change you?

       **Point them to the four ways Paul defines its impact on believers: 1) Teaching – reveals to you what is true. 2) Rebuking – informs you in what ways your**

**choices do not align with God's. 3) Correction – realigns your heart with God's goodness. 4) Training (literally 'go to the gym') in righteousness – guides you in the actual practice of 'putting on Christ.' This last purpose of study is what is meant by "How shall we then live?"**

- How will this help guide you in participating in conforming to his likeness?

  **Equips us for every good (*agathos* - goodness of character) work.**

- Four questions to ask of the text:

  1) What does this passage reveal to me about God?

  2) How does this encourage me in my love and worship of God?

  3) How does this change how I understand who I am?

  4) What action step should I take in response to what I learned?

- Set time aside for this discipline. Determine, with counsel, what else you need to learn to be able to gain knowledge of God.

  **Encourage them to be further discipled in the study of Scripture. Point them to a next level class available through your church or to an online training course that would benefit them.**

- Learn from leaders by listening to their doctrinal teaching: Ephesians 4:11-16

a. Why is this important for you?

**Remind them that Jesus gave these leaders to the church for just this purpose—so believers would not be confused (tossed to and fro by waves or carried by every wind) because of human cunningness designed to destroy their faith in God's goodness.**

b. When and how will you practice this kind of study?

**Discuss the various means available – sermons by their pastor, podcasts, internet teachers, reading books on doctrine, Bible studies/classes, etc.**

5. **For the Facilitator: Practice the above questions in class using Romans 12:1-2. This is to help prepare the participants to understand how to study the passage assigned as homework.**

**Homework:** Practice this discipline using Psalm 46. Ask the four questions of this text. Then reflect on how this passage changes you in light of 2 Timothy 3:14-17.

# Session 5: Do Discipline 3: Self-control

> *Goal of this Session: I will participate with the Spirit to say 'No' to addictive behaviors that are destructive and distract me from intimacy with God, hurting my ability to have people see Christ in me.*

**2 Peter 1:6 "and to knowledge, self-control."**

1. Review Homework: What have you discovered about adding knowledge to your goodness so far?

   **Encourage each participant to answer. The next seven sessions are to encourage them to practice the Do Disciplines so they will grow up further in their faith.**

2. In this session you pursue adding the discipline of self-control to your knowledge. Self-control is one of the major summary terms for Christian conduct (2 Timothy 1:7; Titus 2:6, 12; 1 Peter 4:7), including the final fruit of the Spirit (Galatians 5:22–23). Paul lists it as one of the first things that must characterize leaders in the church (1 Timothy 3:2; Titus 1:8).

   **Have the participants read these verses out loud.**

   - Why do you think the disciples were so concerned for their readers to practice self-control?

   **The early church was making disciples coming from a religious world that openly indulged in all kinds of sexual practices and unrestrained behavior. Although this world included stoicism and asceticism, both of these practices depended on the flesh, not the Spirit. See Colossians 2:16-23 for an example.**

- How does self-control being added to knowledge matter for your faith life?

   **One important point to listen for is that self-control means they are diligently guarding themselves from abandoning the character they have learned about through their study (knowledge of God) which God is using to transform them further into the likeness of Jesus. This diligence means they are guarding their hearts (Proverbs 4:23).**

3. As shown in Luke 4:1-14, what did Jesus teach his disciples about self-control through his life?

   **Self-control for Jesus is recognizing what is his Father's will and choosing to do it His Father's way. Self-control for Jesus meant saying 'No' to an easier or different way. He demonstrates that self-control is necessary if we do not want to miss the will of God for our lives.**

   - Do you think that Jesus really wanted any of the things that the enemy offered?

   **Yes. However, self-control is though desiring things, not choosing to pursue them in a way that does not align with God's will. For example, Jesus knew that he would be lifted up (John 3:15) to draw all humans to him. God's plan led to the cross and resurrection, by which God affirmed him before Israel (Acts 2:29-36) in a way that jumping from the top of the temple would never do.**

   *"Fellow Israelites, I can tell you confidently that the patriarch David died and was buried, and his tomb is here to this day. But he was a prophet and knew that God had promised him on oath that he would place one of his*

*descendants on his throne. Seeing what was to come, he spoke of the resurrection of the Messiah, that he was not abandoned to the realm of the dead, nor did his body see decay. God has raised this Jesus to life, and we are all witnesses of it. Exalted to the right hand of God, he has received from the Father the promised Holy Spirit and has poured out what you now see and hear. For David did not ascend to heaven, and yet he said, "'The Lord said to my Lord: "Sit at my right hand until I make your enemies a footstool for your feet." Therefore let all Israel be assured of this: God has made this Jesus, whom you crucified, both Lord and Messiah."*

- How did Jesus display self-control in his interaction with the enemy?

    **Jesus rebukes the enemy's temptations using the very words of God from Scripture.**

- Why was it important that he did?

    **He had fasted for 40 days in order to prepare himself for the purpose God sent him to do. God also has a purpose for each of His children who are taking this course.**

    **Note: Fasting is a self-control practice. This is a choice to abstain from food or some object that distracts one so he or she can focus on being with God and listening to him uninterruptedly.**

4. What does it mean for you to be self-controlled then?

    **This is a wrap-up question from the previous section. Allow the participants to put this into their own words.**

5. According to Proverbs 25:28, what happens to you when you do not practice self-control?

   **We can be destroyed and rendered helpless against the assaults of the enemy.**

6. Consider Judges 17:6 and 21:25 as an example. What would it do to the community of Jesus if his followers do not practice self-control?

   **The story of Israel throughout the book of Judges was one of continual deterioration as they did whatever they pleased instead of being devoted to God and keeping covenant by following the Law. This led to their domination by another people group until they cried for mercy from God. Then the cycle began all over again, each time Israel sinking lower in their spiritual condition. This parallels the church's history. Suggest modern examples of which you are aware to help the participants see the outcome of not practicing self-control.**

7. What are areas in your life where you are not currently practicing self-control? What impact has this had on you and your circle?

   **This should be a time of reflection, not a time of judgmentalism. Give each person a chance to respond, but do not allow anyone to put them down when they share. At the end of this time, remind them of the Heart Chart, how some symptoms move into addiction mode, not only because of stress and the desire to medicate oneself when under pressure, but also because of the lack of self-control. Remind them this is not where God wills for them to go.**

**Surrender of the underlying causes of the symptoms is His will for them.**

8. What did self-control mean in light of transformation versus reformation?

   **We should not be passive in our embrace of transformational process. Remind them not to try to act good, but diligently do what they are now able to do by the Spirit's power, even when it is challenging.**

9. How do you practice the discipline of self-control?

   - 1 Corinthians 9:27: Choose to discipline yourself. This is about wanting to please God more than doing what you are tempted to do. When you see that you are being pulled, wanting to give in to a temptation, recognize that this is your damaged emotions attaching themselves to damaging behavior that is not in keeping with the character of Jesus. Choose to cooperate with the Spirit by surrendering what is in your heart for healing and freeing.

     **The idea of controlling one's own self presumes at least two things: 1) the presence of something within us that needs to be restrained; 2) the possibility for us to draw on the Spirit's power to restrain it.**

   - Philippians 4:8; Romans 13:14: Decide what you will think about. Determine to clothe yourself with Jesus and not to let the enemy's lies, clothed in culture, fill your mind or they will ignite destructive desires in you. Clothing oneself with Jesus is literally a Spirit empowered decision, similar to dressing oneself in the morning. You chose to 'put on' daily the character of Christ, trusting the Spirit to do this in you. You asked your Father to sustain this in you. You focus your mind on this instead of giving in to the lies of the enemy.

**Ask them what they fill their minds with on a regular basis. It is possible that what they are allowing themselves to think about is giving the enemy an opening to draw them step by step into damaging behavior they never thought they would do. For example, allowing oneself to read or watch sexualized materials, even if it is non-pornographic, can lead to a hunger to go further.**

- James 1:22-25: Hear and obey the Word! You have been given the power through the Spirit already to be self-controlled, so read the Bible to see how God wants you to live.

**Remind them again that they have already been empowered by the Spirit to obey. Encourage them to appropriate this power.**

- Titus 2:11-12: Say 'No!' to all temptations and ungodliness by the grace given to you. This involves allowing the Spirit and Scripture to show you the way the enemy has created traps that can draw you in if you remain unaware. There are three ways to practice saying 'No!'

**This is a critical step of obedience.**

   o  Literally say 'No!' out loud to the enemy.

   o  Follow Jesus' example in Luke 4:1-14 by reminding the enemy of what God said in His Word.

   **Remind them that grace means the empowering presence of the Spirit.**

- There are times when the best strategy is flight, like Joseph fleeing Potiphar's wife in Genesis 39: 11–12.

   **Share with participants the kinds of temptations that you have handled in one or more of these three ways. This will help them see that temptation is a common weapon of the enemy. Tell them that it is not a sin to be tempted, but if they do not say 'No!' to the temptation, it will overcome their ability to resist it and they will sin.**

10. **For the Facilitator: End this session by encouraging them to spend time practicing the Done Discipline of Rest—being with God without an agenda—which will allow them to deepen their relationship with God. This will also strengthen their desire to resist temptation.**

**Homework:** Solomon warns his son to guard his heart in Proverbs 4:23. List out what temptations you know you are drawn toward. Next ask yourself what you are doing, where you're going or how you have opened your mind that gives strength to these temptations. Then write out next to each what God has said. Finally, plan to appropriate the Spirit's power to say 'No!' to these temptations.

# Session 6: Do Discipline 4: Perseverance

> *Goal of this Session: I will be steadfast in the face of temptation and discouragement so that I will not quit when life in the fallen world becomes painful or threatening.*

**2 Peter 1:6 "and to self-control, perseverance."**

1. Review Homework: What have you discovered about adding self-control to your knowledge so far?

   **Encourage each participant to answer.**

2. This session focuses on the discipline of perseverance. What do you understand perseverance to mean in light of 1 Peter 4:12-17?

   **Perseverance means continuing to live out goodness even when it is hard and people oppose you. Perseverance is not about triumphing over adversity; it is about being faithful in goodness when facing the test of adversity. Another word used in place of perseverance is steadfastness, the characteristic of a person who is unswerving from his deliberate purpose and his loyalty to faith and piety by even the greatest trials and sufferings.**

   - What does Romans 5:3-5 tell you about perseverance?

     **God uses suffering to produce perseverance in believers as part of the process of restoring the character of Christ in us, which is the nature of our hope. Suffering includes:**

1) temptation to sin; 2) verbal abuse; 3) violence against you; 4) threats; 5) destruction or theft of possessions; 6) prison—any and all of which can lead to the temptation to quit.

- What does the early disciples' response to persecution in Acts 5:27-42 also tell you about perseverance?

    **Remind the participants that persecution and temptation is not an everyday experience. You may have no idea when it will come or where it will come from. But when it comes, you need to have already decided and readied yourself to persevere. This passage demonstrates the training aspect of this discipline. They were trained in this discipline by being with Jesus, some even failing the test at first (Peter's denials, for example), but not giving in to their failures. Training literally means 'going to the gym.' People work out at the gym because they know they need strength and endurance. This is exactly the way you prepare yourself for perseverance.**

- What does 1 Peter 4:1-4 tell you about why you need to add perseverance to your self-control?

    **This passage points out that the abuse you may suffer often comes at the hands of people you know and with whom you may have engaged in sinful activities in the past. History since Jesus shows that they are capable and willing to use the power of the government to carry out their desire to persecute.**

3. Read the following statement:

*Right now, in the safety of your fellowship, you may not be thinking about what would induce you to consider giving up your faith. You may be thoroughly convinced nothing will shake you. You may have had doubts, but in recent times you have quieted those doubts through connection with other believers and a sense of wellbeing. So, ask yourself, although you do not think it possible here, what might happen in life that would cause you to question the presence of God and His love for you?*

- Have you or someone you know ever thought about giving up on faith?

    **Allow all who need to talk about this. Remind them this is a common issue among all believers, not just weak ones.**

- What do you make of the common reasons believers might want to give up?

    **Use this question to help them identify places where they may already be struggling in their faith.**

    o Psalm 28:1 Confused about what God is doing in your situation or why He has not answered you.

    **This is more common than believers think. 'Unanswered' prayers in a moment of crisis or feelings of desertion are issues that the enemy exploits to crush believers. Teach them that there is no such thing as unanswered prayer, because God lives in them and has given them every spiritual blessing in Christ already.**

    o Psalm 92:5 Discouragement.

**This is caused by the believer's loss of focus on the goodness and love of God by focusing on his or her vulnerabilities and inabilities.**

- 2 Timothy 4:10 Love of the world over Jesus.

    **Sometimes what the enemy offers a believer seems better than the sacrifice God asks of him or her. This is the kind of temptation the enemy uses to get around what the believer thought were settled beliefs.**

- Personal attacks that seem to indicate God is unhappy with you.

    **Brainstorm with the participants what kinds of attacks might be included. Include: 1) Persecution; 2) Family rejection; 3) Severe and continual temptation, 4) Sickness; 4) Financial hardship/poverty; 5) Job loss; 6) Social rejection.**

4. The book of Hebrews was written to a group of believers who were considering giving up on faith in Jesus. What was the nature of the writer's encouragement for them in Hebrews 10:32-35?

    **The writer of Hebrews encouraged them to return to their eternal perspective about suffering. He reminds us that this present life is not the whole of our life—that God is watching and has promised to reward us in the coming life if we persevere.**

5. According to Hebrews 5:7-8, what did Jesus teach his disciples about this issue through his own life?

**Jesus' life was an ongoing illustration to his disciples about perseverance. He did not have to put up with persecution and humiliation. He chose to do it. And God strengthened him is his obedience. This is a reminder that we who follow Jesus should look to him for how we should live. This will be coming up next in the practice of this discipline. We also need to look at how he responded to being nailed to the cross in Luke 23:34. Jesus shows that perseverance is not just enduring through a tough time but reflecting the goodness of God while doing it.**

6. How do you do the discipline of perseverance?

    **Remind them that these are Spirit-empowered training exercises they need to practice *before* endurance is required. Also tell them that one of the great benefits of the discipline of perseverance is the ability to bounce back from the down times, not let them discourage you or make you quit. But perseverance is only half of it. The other half is looking to the Lord to give you the strength to see things through.**

    - Romans 8:35-39 Hold onto God's love. Say to yourself, "God has not changed His mind about His love for me, no matter how hard this is."

        **The list Paul gives of reasons people might think they are separated from God's love—trouble, hardship, etc.—is redefined by Paul as the unfortunate outcome of living in a world affected by the Fall. Remind the participants that they need to embed into their hearts the truth that nothing can or will separate them from God's love.**

- 1 John 4:16 In addition to the previous, live in (literally 'inside') God's love. Revel in His love because you cannot stop God from loving you and you are created to enjoy Him.

  **Here is where persevering is strengthened by both the knowledge of the truth about God, and by *knowing* God (resting in Him).**

- 1 Peter 5:8 Be aware of who the enemy is and what he is trying to do to you. Say to the enemy, "The Lord rebuke you." (Jude 1: 9)

  **The goal of this discipline is not to fixate on the enemy nor try to beat him with our own strength, since the Father has already defeated him by the cross.**

- Hebrews 12:1-3 Fix your eyes on Jesus.

  **This is the most powerful part of this discipline. It has to do with how the believer is empowered by the Spirit to see his or her world. Are you focused on those who have power in the world or on the One who has all power? This part of the discipline is an extension of the Done Disciplines. Being with Jesus to know him, appropriating Jesus' power and trusting Jesus' love. This is exactly what Paul meant in Colossians 3:1-3, when some teachers at that church were undermining their faith by trying to get them to practice asceticism over trusting the Spirit's work in them to make them righteous. Christ is your life!**

**Homework:** List out the areas in your past where you feel you failed to live righteously. After making this list, spend time before

God meditating on Jesus' power. Ask God to focus your eyes—your mind and heart—on what Jesus is able to do so you will gain confidence in him instead of trying to fix yourself in your own strength.

# Session 7: Do Discipline 5: Godliness

> *Goal of this Session: I choose to focus my heart on loving God back so that I will do what He wants me to do, thus preventing persecution and temptation from being the story of my spiritual life.*

**2 Peter 1:6 "and to perseverance, godliness."**

1. Review Homework: What have you discovered about adding perseverance to your self-control so far?

   **Encourage each participant to answer.**

2. This session is about adding the discipline of godliness to your perseverance. Godliness is a term often used to characterize what we should be as believers. This point is so deeply held that those who do not follow Jesus use it to accuse believers who they think are not measuring up of hypocrisy. It is therefore important for your spiritual life that you understand the nature of this discipline so you will live a life that glorifies your Father.

   - What is godliness?
   **Because this is a common word used by the church, people often think they know what it means. But its definition can be unclear to many believers. As the facilitator, you will probably need to guide them to the answer. Godliness is about living out your life with a heart focused on what God wants for you and through you. Godliness (*eusebeia* from eú = good + sébomai = worship, venerate, pay homage) is literally "good worship" which reflects the desire to live with a sense of**

God's presence and motivated by love to please Him in all things we say, do and think. This is the same way Jesus said his followers would be motivated to obey in John 14:15 "If you love me, keep my commands." Spirit-produced godliness reflects the nature of God Himself instead of the temporary, earth–bound 'goodness' of men. The outcome of godliness is it causes us to hate what sin does to us and others.

- How is this different from the idea of piety?

Piety is associated with practicing a set of spiritual behaviors, such as prayer, giving alms to the poor, fasting and even being devoutly religious—all good things in themselves. But the *discipline* of godliness is about training yourself to be alert every day to what God wants, even when life is difficult, and then doing it.

- Why do you need to add it to your perseverance?

Perseverance can lead a believer to focus on survival spiritual warfare and turn you inward and away from what God is able to do through you. An example of this is the church of Ephesus in Revelation 2:2-5. *"I know your deeds, your hard work and your perseverance. I know that you cannot tolerate wicked people, that you have tested those who claim to be apostles but are not, and have found them false. You have persevered and have endured hardships for my name, and have not grown weary. <u>Yet I hold this against you: You have forsaken the love you had at first.</u> Consider how far you have fallen! Repent and do the things you did at first. If you do not repent, I will come to you and remove your lampstand from its place."* The believers in this church demonstrated that you can be doing well in persevering and lose your way in the matter of godliness. Godliness counterbalances this tendency so that you are able to return good for evil, and impact people around you with the good news about Jesus.

3. How does Paul demonstrate the relationship between perseverance and godliness in 2 Corinthians 4:7-11?

   Even while persevering through the difficulties of living out your faith, you can still emerge secure in your life's purpose, to display the life of Jesus. This is possible by God's all-surpassing power, not our feeble attempts at it.

   - What are some difficult circumstances that might challenge you to fail to practice godliness?

     It is easier to be godly in a group intensive than in life. Help the participants to pre-think what they might do in difficult circumstances, which can prepare them when such troubles come at them. Have some examples in mind, such as: 1) the death of one of your children; 2) the murder of a person you love by an evil person; 3) being fired from your job due to the prejudice of your overseer; 4) discovering a trusted friend sexually abused your child; 5) you discover your mate is unfaithful to you. Remind them that the enemy is prowling like a roaring lion, seeking whom he can devour. The goal of this question is to allow them to see why they need to discipline themselves in godliness—so that it becomes natural for them to respond with godliness when life is hard.

- This is not something you can fake! One of the characteristics Paul uses to describe false believers in his day is found in 2 Timothy 3:1-13. It is possible for people to appear to be godly who are not. People often adopt the language and outward activities of godliness without ever becoming godly. Why do they do this?

  **Paul states here that the motivation for these people is a desire to have influence and want to take advantage of others through faking godliness. They even seek to take leadership (=teachers) among God's people (Jannes and Jambres) but are rejected by God. These are people who do not truly believe in the reality of God—and that He not only sees but stores up judgment against their behavior (Romans 2:5). Point out that Paul's teaching was tested over and over again by persecution and yet Paul himself demonstrated true godliness under persecution in contrast to the false teachers' counterfeits.**

4. What did Jesus teach his disciples about being godly under pressure in Luke 22:47-51?

   **This is just one of many incidences where Jesus demonstrated his godliness while dealing with hostility, in this case, his arrest which led to crucifixion. Much of Jesus' teaching on this subject was demonstrated to his disciples through his life actions, supplemented by his teaching. This was the way a disciple learned from a Rabbi. The disciples did not merely take notes of what Jesus said, but observed what he *did* so they would know how they were to live. See John 21:25. "Jesus did many other things as well. If every one of them were written down, I suppose that even the**

whole world would not have room for the books that would be written."

5. So, what does the practice of godliness in the world look like according to Jesus' words in Matthew 23:23?

**Guide the participants in seeing the difference between God's heart and the religious practices people do to show their godliness. The hallmark of godliness in God's character is justice (on behalf of those who are oppressed), mercy on those who need mercy, and faithfulness in keeping covenant with us.**

- In what practical ways should these be lived out in your own life?

    **1) Justice: There is a tendency to ignore Jesus' training in doing justice, which is a constant theme of the Old Testament prophets as well. Explore this with the participants.**

    **2) Mercy: Discuss mercy from the point of view of Jesus asking the Father to forgive those crucifying him in Luke 23:34. "Jesus said, "Father, forgive them, for they do not know what they are doing."" How should we show mercy in a world that attacks our faith and denies biblical values, even seeking to infuse their own values into our children?**

    **3) Faithfulness: What does it mean to be faithful when challenged by God's truths that contradict cultural traditions, which is what Jesus is pointing out to the Pharisees? Remind them that all cultures in the world were built by people affected by the Fall.**

6. What do Paul's concluding instructions in 1 Thessalonians 5:12- 22 add to your understanding of the practice of godliness?

   **This list includes many every day practices of godliness, mostly to be practiced within the body of Christ: 1) respect for God's servants; 2) live at peace with others; 3) warn those whose actions are hurting the body; 4) encourage those who struggle spiritually; 5) help the weak in faith; 6) be patient; 7) do not return evil for evil, but strive to do good to each other; 8) worship well through rejoicing, prayer and thanksgiving; 9) do not quench the Spirit; 10) test what is proclaimed in God's name without condemning it out of hand; 11) hold on to good, reject all evil.**

7. Perhaps you are not currently doing some of the above practices Jesus and Paul mentioned. This indicates the need to discipline yourself in godliness. Consider the following statement.

   *Train yourself to be godly. For physical training is of some value, but godliness has value for all things, holding promise for both the present life and the life to come.* (Godliness is a discipline you decide to pursue because it has to become a natural aspect of your spiritual life—doing it without having to think about doing it. It is always empowered by the Spirit, but it is an intentional pursuit due to love for God.) *The reason why we toil and struggle so hard is that we have set our hopes on the living God, who is the Savior of all men, and especially of those who believe. (1 Timothy 4:7 & 10)*

   - According to this, what is the motivation and outcome for training yourself in godliness?

     **The motivation they should see in this is the *hope* (which means the certainty of our complete restoration to who**

were created to be) brought about by the demonstration of God's power in saving us. The outcome is to be *ourselves*—to be able to naturally act godly instead of failing at it or worse, faking it.

8. How do you discipline yourself in the practice of godliness?

- Romans 6:19. Choose to surrender to righteousness.

    **Choosing is the only ability we have as humans, but we don't have the power to carry out our choice. In the past, we have chosen to surrender to impurity and it has drawn us down. Now choose to surrender to righteousness and the Spirit's power will draw you on into godliness.**

- Luke 6:40: Study the life of Jesus as recorded in the Gospels. Learn how Jesus demonstrated godliness by asking the following questions.

    **Jesus is using the Greek word *katartizo*, which means "to prepare, to perfect for its full use, to bring to its proper condition." He is our Rabbi. We need to see what he did and then imitate him—again, by the Spirit's power.**

    o How did he respond to opposition?
    o What did he say that encouraged, warned, helped?
    o What did he do that changed the situation, challenged the hearers, brought hope to the onlookers?
    o How am I to imitate him?

Practice this in class by studying Jesus' life in Mark 4:35-41.

**This should be an interesting study for the participants. What Jesus did in the boat at first demonstrated his complete faith in God to take care of him in the storm, so he slept. What the disciples did in the boat showed that they lacked faith that God was going to take care of them in the storm. What are the takeaways from this passage?**

- **Even when his disciples have small faith, Jesus still responds. But he will also use the moment to challenge them to grow up some more in their faith.**
- **It's okay to fear the Lord. Jesus, by his miraculous act of stilling the storm is revealing he is God (see Psalm 89:8-9).**
- **Disciples grow in faith when they do what their Rabbi is doing. To imitate him, they should have laid down and slept also!**
- **How does the participant imitate him? By learning to respond in faith in whatever life circumstance he or she finds themselves.**

- Mark 4:40: Meditate on why you might be afraid. Consider what fears the enemy is using to currently keep you from living in a godly manner.

**The story of Jesus calming the storm has several undercurrents the participants may not know. 1) The storm, which so petrified the disciples, many of whom were experienced with boats and fishing for a living on**

the Sea of Galilee, was not just a coincidence, but a testing of their faith. 2) Jesus, their Rabbi, sleeping during the storm. They, being his disciples, should have done what their Rabbi was doing if they were consistent in following his example. Instead, they panicked, woke him and demanded to know what he was going to do about the situation. After demonstrating his power over the wind and waves, Jesus asked them about their fear and faith. The point he is making is that their fear was overwhelming their ability to trust him—and thus, God. Jesus was not going to drown no matter what the enemy threw at him. The application is this—we as his disciples need to discern what fears might keep us from fully imitating the godliness we see in Jesus and submit those fears to him so that our faithfulness will grow.

**Homework:** This week, read John 1-8. What did Jesus do and say that teaches godliness?

# Session 8: Do Discipline 6: Mutual Affection

> *Goal of this Session: I will meet the physical and emotional needs of those who belong to God because we are family.*

**2 Peter 1:7 "and to godliness, mutual affection."**

1. What have you discovered about adding godliness to your perseverance so far?

   **Encourage each participant to answer.**

2. This session is about adding mutual affection to your godliness. The word for mutual affection is *philadelphia*, after which the city Philadelphia is named. It literally means 'sibling friendship.'

   - Why do you see the addition of mutual affection as important to your godliness?

     **Godliness, which is *living out your life with a heart focus on what God wants for you and through you*, needs an objective. In this and the following session, the participants will see two focuses that God wills for them to develop in their spiritual life: 1) showing love to their spiritual family members; 2) showing love to those outside the faith (next week's focus). Godliness without these objectives devolves into personal piety instead of an active demonstration of God's love.**

   - How were you treated by your biological family? Did you have a good or bad family life?

**This personal question may shed light on the challenge the participant may have in showing mutual affection. If they grew up in a loveless and damaged family, they may not have experienced kindness and care.**

- Do you find it harder in your life to get along with your friends or your family members? Why?

**This background question is to allow you, the facilitator, a glimpse of what may make this easier or harder for the participant to master. A bad family homelife often transfers into how they might avoid and dislike some of their siblings in Christ. This often is due to the damaged emotions behind their unfinished business. Talk about this if anyone admits to a troubled upbringing. This idea carries over into the next question.**

- Is there someone you have cut out of your spiritual family because you found them difficult?

**Remind them that not only do *they* have to deal with their unfinished business with God, but so do all their other family members in the Lord.**

3. What happens when a church does not practice mutual affection? Explore Corinth Church and the issues of division and disrespect, among other issues of sinful behavior towards God.

**Point out that Paul wrote some of his most profound transformational statements in his two letters to the Corinthians, including 1 Corinthians 15:9-10, 2 Corinthians 3:17-18 and 12:9-10. (Look these up and share them in class.) The Corinth church knew the transformational gospel, but failed to grasp its power due**

to their immaturity and self centeredness. Use this section to help them apply these same sinful behaviors to modern believers, so they can see the damage that is caused by the lack of mutual affection. All of these are caused by the sins of pride and anger.

- 1 Corinthians 1:10-13 Factions due to arrogance.

    **This can be seen when we are divided into groups over disagreements about who is important and about minor doctrinal differences. This is driven by the sin of pride.**

- 1 Corinthians 4:14-18 Disrespect for their spiritual father Paul.

    **This is seen when we are lacking appreciation, and worse—expressing underserved and harsh judgment on spiritual leaders God gave to congregations.**

- 1 Corinthians 6:1-8 Lawsuits against each other.

    **This is seen when we have the inability to reconcile or mediate problems between ourselves as believers.**

- 1 Corinthians 8:1-13 Insensitivity over issues of dietary laws of others.

    **It is arrogance to believe our way is God's way, when in fact, the differences we look down upon are mainly cultural and of not eternal importance.**

- 1 Corinthians 10:23-24 Using spiritual slogans to act self-centeredly and sinfully.

**This is excusing sinful activity in the congregation because 'God allows it' and He is so forgiving that it does not matter what His people do.**

- 1 Corinthians 11:17-23 Exclusion of the poor from the Lord's Supper by those who are rich.

  **We need to be aware of social and economic class distinctions that allow believers to look down on each other. This is also a human cultural response, instead of the response of people belonging to Jesus' kingdom.**

- 1 Corinthians 14:1-5 (All of chapters 12-14) Disrupting worship to show off.

  **This happens when believers make themselves the center of attention so that others 'know' that they are more special in God's sight.**

- What do you see in this list that has affected your own faith community?

  **Give them time to reflect on this question before they answer. It can be painful to admit some of the same problems exist in their own fellowship.**

4. Of course, differences do happen between believers. Differences do not mean we worship a different God or deny the truth about Jesus, the central truths of the gospel or should act in ways to purposely hurt other believers. Differences mean we may approach certain aspects of our faith differently, follow certain traditions or cultural practices that feel uncomfortable to other believers, because we believe doing so honors God and our leaders. Instead of abandoning mutual affection between us

and these believers, how does Paul direct that these differences be addressed in Romans 14:10-21?

**This is an important teaching. The Jewish and Gentile believers in the church of Rome certainly had different perspectives about what constituted righteous behavior in certain areas of their faith life. But notice that these had no eternal value in the eyes of God. Paul is teaching them to not judge their fellow believers based on *preferences*, but to leave that decision to God at His bema judgment. Instead, they should do all they can to minimize their differences, and to seek *not* to make those who are of a different mind uncomfortable. To practice mutual affection!**

- What are some practices of other believers that bother you?

    **This is a personal question meant to draw them to making application of the above truths.**

- How can you show such people mutual affection?

    **Encourage them to supply actions steps here, not merely abstract ideas.**

5. To be clear, according to 1 Peter 1:22, what is the foundational reason you need to practice this discipline?

**Explain to the participants that they are not doing this in response to others showing them mutual affection, but out of gratitude for God's love which resulted in saving them from their sins. He did not just save them; He placed them into a fellowship for mutual benefit and their growth in love. See also 1 Thessalonians 4:9-10.**

6. Of all the stories recorded about Jesus and his disciples, the one that brings clarity to the discipline of mutual affection is found in John 13:1-17.

   - What is the lesson Jesus was teaching them about mutual affection?

   **Serving each other, loving each other, paying attention to each other's needs. It takes humility!**

   - What does 'washing each other's feet' look like in the body of Christ?

   **This section of verses is to help the participants expand their understanding of mutual affection. Again, ask them to suggest concrete actions they can take.**

     o Acts 4:32 Making sure their needs are met.
     o Hebrews 10:24 Spur each other on toward love and good deeds.
     o 2 Timothy 4:9-11 Ministry of Presence.

     **This is by far the one action many believers fail to understand. Sometimes, just being there when people need you, even when you have nothing you think you can offer, is a matter of washing another's feet.**

     o 1 John 3:17 Benevolence.
     o 1 Thessalonians 5:11 Encourage other believers.
     o Galatians 6:1-2 Restoration of those caught in sin.

- - Ephesians 4:32 Forgive those who offend you just like God forgave you.
  - Hebrews 10:32-33 Stand with those who suffer.
  - 2 Corinthians 7:3 Do not give up on a family member.
  - Compassion and encouragement when they struggle with unfinished business – concern for their soul.
- Who exactly are you supposed to do this for?

  **This is a reminder to them to take care of other believers.**

- Are you aware of the above practices taking place in your fellowship? Has any other believer washed your feet?

  **Expect them all to answer. If they are not aware, encourage them to be the initiators of these practices.**

7. How do you practice the discipline of mutual affection?

   **Help them recognize that this discipline requires outward focus instead of inward focus. Emphasize the first aspect of this discipline, the need to be part of a fellowship of believers. It is impossible to do this discipline otherwise.**

   - Hebrews 10:25 You cannot do this discipline alone. You have to be part of a fellowship of believers!
     - Who are you in community with currently?
   - Colossians 3:12 Clothe yourself! Surrender to the Spirit's developmental power to form these characteristics in you, all of which are focused on how to treat others and practice them on people in your community.

**Clothing oneself has been one of the underlying truths of this whole intensive. This list from Paul in Colossians allows us to continue to focus on what it means to be conformed into Jesus' likeness, because these are his characteristics.**

- First understand what these characteristics are.

    1) What does compassion look like?

        **Caring for people who need to be cared for, no matter how difficult they are.**

    2) What does kindness look like?

        **Acting toward people in ways that meet their deepest needs emotionally as well as physically.**

    3) What does humility look like?

        **To not consider yourself better or more worthy of God's love than anyone else.**

    4) What does gentleness look like?

        **To keep one's power under control so that people do not get hurt by your actions or words.**

    5) What does patience look like?

        **To be willing to endure with a person until he or she arrives at wisdom or healing.**

- Here is a way to do this:

    1) Realize your need to be clothed in this way.

2) Respond by appropriating the Spirit's power to be that.

3) Act in faith in that power.

- Galatians 6:9-10: Keep doing good and do not quit even when it is tiring.

**Mutual affection sometimes is another form of perseverance.**

**Homework:** Look at the list in #5. Decide what I will do this week to show mutual affection. Appropriate the Spirit's power for this and then do it.

# Session 9: Do Discipline 7: Love

> *Goal of this Session: I will allow my mind and heart to be changed so that I love lost people, even those who are hard to love because they hate me and seek to do me harm.*

**2 Peter 1:7 "and to mutual affection, love"**

1. Review Homework: What have you discovered about adding mutual affection to your godliness so far?

2. Who do you hate?

   **This opening question is to get the participants thinking about the people that they may not want to love. Encourage them to be real and raw in their responses, so they will seek real help from this discipline.**

3. This session is about the discipline of love. This is about 'agape,' which is the kind of love that God shows us. This love is a second focus for living out the practice of godliness.

   - What does Peter mean when he speaks of adding love to mutual affection?

     **Agape is a will choice rather than an emotional or value choice. Believers tend to be selective in to whom they show mutual affection. Love broadens your horizons and opens your eyes to those who need to be shown love.**

   - What is the difference between these two disciplines?

     **Mutual affection is largely focused on those who belong to Jesus, whereas the discipline of love focuses on those**

who are outside God's family—treating them lovingly in spite of their disdain for you or loving them regardless of their behavior. This truth has deep implications for how you proclaim the gospel in the world.

- How does 1 John 3:18 guide you in how to practice this discipline?

   Believers think they are practicing love when they do not do or say hateful or harmful things toward the lost. But true agape is to take action steps—not begrudgingly or out of duty—that mirror Jesus' acts toward those who were lost when he was on earth. This would include feeding the hungry, clothing the ragged, visiting the sick or those in jail and serving people who need help.

- Why is love a Do Discipline?

   This is about becoming a person possessed by love, a loving person rather than a person who tries to be loving. Peter, echoing Jesus, is saying, 'Do not try to love your enemies, but become the kind of person who finds it natural to extend love to them.' This idea is imbedded in all of the Do Disciplines. Remember that agape is the act of the will to love, not a response to the worthiness, beauty or attributes of the one needing love.

4. Jesus taught his disciples many lessons on this issue. One of his most profound parables, The Good Samaritan in Luke, focuses on what it means to love your neighbor—those who are not part of your family—as yourself.

   - Why did Jesus tell this parable in the first place?

This parable was in response to a religious leader seeking to justify himself—trying to find a loophole in Jesus' comprehensive response to what the law of God was all about. If you love others well, you will fulfill the law. The religious leaders of Jesus' day believed that there were a lot of people excluded from God's love, therefore they did not have to love them either.

- Who needed to be loved?

  **The broken, the damaged, the rebellious, the lost. Those, Jesus once said, who were sick and in need of a doctor.**

- Why did the priest and Levite not show him love?

  **They had other priorities they thought were higher. Both were probably concerned that, if he died while they tended him, they would be religiously unclean, a big deal for a priest and Levite, who served in the temple.**

- Why did the Samaritan show him love?

  **Because the man was helpless.**

- What form did this love take?

  **He took the time and effort to bind his wounds, get him to safety and pay for his expenses out of his own pocket.**

- What do you understand was Jesus' point?

  **Love for others is not a conditional choice, it is a lifestyle. If a person you might think of as ungodly (the Jewish view of Samaritans) can show love, then this is**

**what Jesus meant by being a neighbor. You cannot duck this and claim to be righteous.**

5. Jesus is more than our Savior. He is also our teacher in how to love. How did Jesus himself show love to those who did not deserve love?

   **Look at these passages together and have them draw out the lessons of love.**

   - Luke 19:1-10 Zacchaeus.

     **Do not let them miss Jesus' willingness to lose popularity to go eat at a 'sinner's' home.**

   - Luke 23:34 The soldiers nailing him to the cross.

     **Forgiveness in the face of great cruelty.**

   - Mark 10:17-22 The rich young ruler.

     **Loving patience with those who are arrogant.**

6. There are reasons believers struggle to practice this kind of love for their enemies. Consider the following:

   **Guide the participants to apply these reasons personally instead of keeping them abstract.**

   - Romans 5:12

     **Believers are battling the effects of the Fall within themselves just like every other human.**

   - 1 Corinthians 1:22-25

     **We have been raised in one or another human culture, including our personal family culture, we struggle with**

the beliefs and attitudes those cultures have taught us. It is not easy to cast off the influences of a culture affected by the Fall and show loving kindness to nonbelievers, even those who are within our culture, much less outside it.

- Because of one or more of these reasons, what needs to happen within you for you to be able to love your enemies?

    This is a *metanoia* issue—to change your mind about who is in charge of you. Jesus is our savior and master. We want our minds to align with his (which is empowered by the Spirit) and to surrender our rights to hate, to him.

    Note: You may be familiar with *metanoia* being interpreted as repentance or to change one's mind about sin. But the human problem since the Fall was we chose to reject God's reign over us, falsely thinking we can reign over ourselves. Repenting of this false idea and surrendering to His reign empowers our ability to love our enemies.

7. What practical ways are shown in the following Scriptures that we should love.

    **Ask the participants for life examples of each of the following.**

    - Matthew 5:43-48 Pray for them and love transformationally instead of transactionally.

        We have learned from human interaction that love is transactional. That you have to give love to get love. This is not the love God is empowering us to have.

- 1 Corinthians 13:4-7 Actively allow love to shape your demeanor towards others.

    **Agape is about responding calmly when faced with difficulties, sacrificing without complaining, and waiting patiently. This type of love is selfless and is for the preservation of relationships and the development of another person.**

- Romans 12:17-21 Return good for evil.

    **This is particularly important in light of cultural wars that can tempt believers to hate their opponents.**

- Romans 13:8-10 Do not deliberately sin against your neighbor.

- 1 Peter 4:8 Love them in a way that overlooks their sins.

    **God's love empowers people to turn away from sin (covers). It does not approve of sin or excuse it but recognizes that how we (or God) handles sinners draws people to forgiveness and forsaking sin.**

8. How should we see people that we normally would hate?

    **We should see them with compassion because they are broken instead of enemies. And they're not beyond hope of salvation. Consider how Jesus responded to the thief on the cross and ask the Spirit to empower you to respond the same.**

9. How do you practice the discipline of love?

**Much of the practice of the discipline of love is covered in #8. But the two following exercises go to the heart of this practice.**

- Matthew 5:44-45 Make a list of people by name that you do not love and begin praying for them and praying also that God would give you agape for them.

  **Starting this list will be their homework. Direct them to pray first that God would empower their love for their enemies.**

- Matthew 9:35-38 Share the gospel with those who you see with compassion.

  **This is the most important part of this discipline. Discuss with them what is their knowledge about sharing their witness. You should direct those who have never learned to do this to an appropriate evangelizing training class.**

**Homework:** Begin making a list of kinds of people you find yourself either actively hating or lacking compassion for. Pray that God would change your heart.

# Session 10: Effective and Productive

> *Goal of this Session: I will go forward on my faith journey diligently pursuing these characteristics because I want my life actions to glorify God through the fruit it produces.*

**2 Peter 1:8 "They will keep you from being ineffective and unproductive."**

1. Review Homework: What have you discovered about adding love to your mutual affection so far?

   **Encourage each participant to answer.**

2. Revisit the seven Do Disciplines.

   **These opening questions are to allow them to reflect on how far along they are in adding to their faith. Encourage those who are struggling to implement these disciplines. Remind them that Peter is teaching these practices because they are integral to the work of God in conforming us into the likeness of Jesus.**

   - Which are the ones you find more challenging at this point? Why?

   - Which ones are the most rewarding so far? How are they rewarding?

3. This last session explores the encouragement that Peter gives to those who are diligent in adding the seven practices to their faith. These seven define what it means to be a kingdom servant. Before we examine his words, read what Paul says about serving in Colossians 3:23-24.

**A kingdom servant will understand that on his or her faith journey, they are always in the service of their King. Explore with those in the class whether they have understood this aspect of putting their faith in Jesus.**

- What is the difference between being a regular churchgoer and a kingdom servant?

**Many believers view themselves as churchgoers, which is a contradiction. Believers cannot *go* to church because they *are* the church, biblically speaking. But more to the point, Jesus calls his followers into the kingdom, where they are empowered by the Spirit to serve to the glory of God. This is an important distinction, because it is how a believer understands who he or she is in Christ that guides their decisions in living out the faith. A churchgoer will often focus their faith solely on what happens inside the church building. A kingdom servant will see serving the Father in whatever ways He opens for them beyond the walls of the church building—in their neighborhood, workplace, etc.—as their role in the kingdom.**

- Were you ever taught the difference between these two or is this the first time you heard that there is a difference?

**Do not be surprised if this truth is new for many in the class. Take a few minutes to explain 'kingdom' as Jesus used the term in Matthew 4:17 and throughout his ministry on earth. It means 'God's right to reign over all He has created.' Even if humans have and do reject His reign, He still reigns over all nations and people. He is allowing them to experience the impact of the Fall so they will realize through its effects their need of His**

salvation, or, as Paul puts it in 2 Corinthians 5:18-19, their need to be reconciled to Him, resubmitting themselves to His reign. This is the basic meaning of 'repent.' Through Adam's and Eve's choice of eating of the tree of good and evil, humans rejected God's reign over them. Repenting is to 'change one's mind' about who has the right to be in charge of you. For those who have put their faith in Jesus, they have become his servants. We are serving him now by seeing the lost with compassion, aware that we are demonstrating His mercy and grace to save even the worst of sinners, as Paul describes himself in 1 Timothy 1:15-17.

- If by putting your faith in Jesus you became a kingdom servant, what implications does that have for how you live out your life?

    **Help them process this. The end thought is that all of their life decisions and actions are to be for His glory. Remind them that their faith is not one facet of their lives, but the whole of their lives.**

4. Study this last part of Peter's message carefully. Consider the highlighted notes added to the passage for clarification.

    **This is the focus of the rest of this session.**

    *For if you possess these* **(seven additions to your faith)** *qualities in increasing measure, they will keep you from being ineffective* **(things from which no profit is derived, although they can and ought to be productive, such as fields, trees, gold and silver – they are unprofitable)** *and unproductive* **(fruitless)** *in your knowledge of our Lord Jesus Christ. But whoever does not have them is nearsighted and blind,* *forgetting that they have been cleansed from their past sins* (**unrighteous living people who are afraid of God because they do not know him**). *Therefore, my brothers and sisters, make every effort* (**be diligent**) *to confirm* (**validating that it is true**) *your calling and election* (**actions of God to summon and save you**). *For if you do these things, you will never stumble* (**come to grief, experience disaster, be ruined**), *and you will receive a rich* (**abundant**) *welcome into the eternal kingdom of our Lord and Savior Jesus Christ.*

- Do Peter's words invoke fear in you? Are you personally afraid that you might fail at pleasing God with your life and be judged harshly by Him?

  **Fear is the result of believing and acting on the lies of the enemy, who wants to encourage a sense of failure to measure up to God's demands in the minds of believers. He does this by emphasizing they need to try harder instead of trusting the provision of the empowering Spirit. If you sense there are participants who actually feel the weight of God's judgment over them, because they are still struggling in their faith, this would be a good place to remind them of what they will learn of God's character and love through the Done Disciplines of Rest, Appropriation and Meditating on the love of Christ.**

- In what way is this passage more fully explained in Jesus' parable in Matthew 13:24-30, 36-43 about the wheat and the tares?

  **Jesus, and his disciples who wrote the New Testament, taught there would always be people in his kingdom that did not truly put their faith in him, who would live in**

fellowship with true believers. These are the people Peter is warning, because they are the ones who will be fruitless and unprofitable.

- Why, then is Peter urging you to diligently practice the Do Disciplines?

**Guide the participants to the understanding that there is a benefit to vigorously pursuing a righteous life by the Spirit's power. Peter is not questioning his readers' salvation, but by forewarning them, he is urging them to grow in grace so that the reality of their salvation will be impactful for the kingdom. Have the participants look at 2 Peter 3:17-18, the last verses in this letter to see that this is his point.**

- Consider how being productive and effective matters.
  - How do the Do Disciplines validate your calling and election?

    **Numerous believers wonder if they are truly saved. This is because they stop growing in grace early in their spiritual journey. By being diligent in adding to their faith by the Spirit's power, their maturing spiritual life, moreover, their deeper intimacy with God, confirms the reality of what they have received.**

  - What does Peter mean when he says you will not stumble if you are diligent in practicing these things?

    **He means that you will not end up ruined by foolish life actions and find yourself at life's end grieving because you chose unwisely how you would live out your life.**

- We will come back to the issue of receiving a rich welcome into the eternal kingdom. But now, go deeper: Does it really matter to you that you are effective and productive in your faith? If so, why?

  **This is a personal reflection question. Do not allow them to give an answer without taking time to reflect.**

5. Read what Jesus taught about becoming fruitful in John 15:1-8.

   - Why does God cut off unfruitful branches and prune good ones?

     **This teaching by Jesus underlies Peter's warning (found in other New Testament passages) that those who do not produce fruit are not really part of His kingdom. They are cut off on the Day God judges the world—a judgment that is different from the bema seat judgment referred to in Question 6 below. Pruning those who are His—an agricultural reference that Jesus' disciples would recognize—is necessary so a vine, plant or tree will continue to produce fruit as it matures. Pruning means cutting off anything in their lives that holds them back, such as things that encumber, sinful habits or distractions that eat up their time.**

   - What do you believe Jesus meant by 'fruit'?

     **While this term can have several meanings, whatever good that results in a believer's life—a righteous walk and/or the conversion of the lost—is produced by being connected with Jesus, filled by his Spirit.**

   - How does a branch produce fruit?

**The branch does not have to work at being fruitful. All it has to do is be connected to a life-giving vine which has roots planted in the right soil. Fruit is the natural outcome. This is what Jesus meant by 'remain in me and I in you' in order to be able to bear fruit. Point out that the participants have come full circle back to being continually filled with the Spirit—that Jesus in us and we in him is the central point of our new covenant relationship. Apart from this relationship, nothing eternal comes out of our lives.**

- In what sense do Jesus' words address your fear of failing at the Do Disciplines?

    **Encourage every person to respond. When they see that by pursuing intimacy with God, they cannot fail to grow in grace, they will lose their needless anxiety over what God thinks of them.**

6. Receiving a rich welcome into Jesus' eternal kingdom is portrayed in the New Testament using the imagery of an athlete receiving his or her prize—usually an olive leaf crown—from the judge of the contest. Read the following verses to get a picture of what they meant—2 Corinthians 5:10; Romans 14:8-10; 1 Corinthians 9:25; 1 Peter 5:4; James 1:12; 2 Timothy 4:8.

    **The goal of this question is to expose the participants to thinking eternally about their life and decisions.**

    - Notice that the English translation calls this welcome the 'judgment seat.' But the original word for judgment is *bema*, which is the seat for the judges of a sporting event, those that hand out the prizes after the games are over. How does knowing this alter your thoughts about God's judgment?

**They should understand that God is a rewarder of those who believe, not a punisher. Refer to Hebrews 11:6 *"And without faith it is impossible to please God, because anyone who comes to Him must believe that He exists and that He rewards those who earnestly seek Him."* If they have been afraid of God's judgment, they need to allow their minds to be renewed with the truth.**

- Knowing that God plans to eternally reward you for being productive and effective, how will this truth help you face the spiritual battle you will experience throughout life?

    **This again is a reflective question. They really will not know its full implications at this moment, but it allows them to set their minds in the right direction.**

- How does knowing this help you to understand what Jesus meant by his promise of peace in John 14:27?

    **Peace is not the lack of warfare in your lives, but God's gift while you strive in warfare. Encourage the participants that God will supply what they need when they need it. Tell them not to live their lives seeking to avoid the battle, or to be afraid, as God has already won through the cross.**

7. You are now at the end of this discipling intensive. But what you have learned does not stop here. As you saw in 2 Peter 3:17-18, these Do Disciplines will equip you to grow in grace. You will learn more about God and yourself as you do these practices; practices which He has empowered you to do by His Spirit. So, take this moment and consider: What will I do to

encourage others in this intensive with me to pursue these practices?

**After they have finished reflecting on this question, have all the participants gather around each person as you pray for them individually. This action is to emphasize their need to encourage and spur each other on in their pursuit of a righteous life, as the writer of Hebrews 10:23-24 said:** *Let us hold unswervingly to the hope we profess, for he who promised is faithful. And let us consider how we may spur one another on toward love and good deeds.*

**Homework:** Sponsor another person you know to go through this discipling intensive.

**Do not skip talking about this with the class. They know people who need to grow up more in their faith.**

Made in the USA
Coppell, TX
30 December 2025

67533270R00059